All Rights Reserved.

No part of this book may be used or reproduced by any means, graphic, electronic, or mechanical, including photocopying, or by any information storage retrieval system without the written permission of the owner except in the case of brief quotations in articles and reviews.

Copyright © 2024 by Tamara Jackson

DEDICATION

This book is dedicated to the unheard and unseen. I hear you and I see you, because I am you!

TABLE OF CONTENTS

Dedication
Introduction
CHAPTER ONE
   Mental/Emotional (Proverbs 23:7)
      Mind
      Heart
      Feelings/Emotions
CHAPTER TWO
   Physical (1 Corinthians 6:19-20)
      Eyes
      Body Image
      Healthy Body
CHAPTER THREE
   Spiritual (John 10:30)
      Spirit
      Soul
      Supernatural Experience Vs. Supernatural Encounter
Conclusion
Authors Bio
References

INTRODUCTION

Have you ever felt overwhelmed and overtaken by life and the events that happen to you? If you've ever come away from a situation feeling depleted and unsure of yourself, I want to encourage you to embark on your own healing journey. In sharing my experiences, I hope to support you as you work on healing your heart. When we experience hurt, shame, and guilt, we often begin to ruminate or start a downward spiral of blaming ourselves and beating ourselves up over what we cannot control. If you have had those experiences, as I have, then this book will help you. I started my healing journey over 20 years ago. I found myself in toxic situations, relationships, and jobs, and I did not understand why they kept happening until I entered counseling, both spiritual and secular. While doing so, I discovered that spirit and secular counseling can co-exist like pain and healing.

Throughout the book, I will refer to God as He because that is how I see God represented in my life. I understand that God is Spirit, and I honor the Spirit of the living God "in spirit and in truth" *(John 4:24)*. While on this healing journey, I experienced an eye-opening moment with God. This supernatural experience was unlike any other I had ever experienced. It was not until after my divorce that I realized I tried to heal myself with the therapeutic skills I previously learned that no longer served me in this phase of my life. When I was hurt before, I would go hang out with my friends, work out like crazy, dance, and have fun to heal myself.

Yes, it worked for a while, but I found myself back on a hamster wheel when I didn't spend enough time finding the root cause of my issues. I didn't understand the pattern of behavior I was doing to myself. I faced what I knew I did with the level of understanding I had about myself. However, I didn't truly give myself enough time to search for myself and heal properly. I felt as if I was on the hamster wheel.

Unfortunately, it was not until I got divorced that I was stuck in all the hurt, feeling guilt and shame, and blaming myself for why it didn't work. I cried, screamed, prayed, and laid prostrate on the floor and the bed (because a sister's back started hurting...LOL). At that moment, I gave up myself and everything I knew to God. I surrendered in a way I never had before.

I blamed myself and asked God every Why I could. During this time of mentally trying to pull myself together and commune with God, the supernatural encounter I experienced with Him demonstratively changed me forever. I had the chance to look back over my entire life. It was one of the most painful moments of my life, and during this time, I saw God and every instance and movement of divine provision, protection, and timing God made on my behalf.

I'd like to mention three principles that were activated during this time: God's divine provision, protection, and timing. These are called Kingdom Principles; seven are listed in Dr. Doral R. Pulley's Wayshower: A New View of Jesus *(Pulley, 2019)*. God used each of these Kingdom Principles to help me during my healing journey. Let's define each of them. **Divine Provision** is when God has already supplied everything we need naturally and spiritually. **Divine Protection** is when God allows us to go through things and experience emotions that are meant to help us on our journey. It doesn't mean you will only experience good things. It does mean that everything you go through will contribute to your healing, and you will be able to give God the glory for your experiences on the other side of it. It may not always feel good, but it will always serve a purpose. **Divine Timing** means that everything in the universe is happening according to God's timing, and everything is happening when it is supposed to happen (*Pulley, 2019*).

God used Divine Provision to ensure I had all my needs met when I was hurt by sending authentic friends for me to talk to, a therapist, and even finances when I needed them. When it came to Divine Protection, God ensured that nothing and no one could come near me when we were spending time together so that He could share with me who I am in Him. Last but certainly not least, Divine Timing; no matter how painful and hard the situation was, I was exactly where I was supposed to be. That pill was extremely hard to swallow because who wants to be in pain? However, in that pain is where God wanted me to be. It was in that pain that I was able to grow and mature in spirit and more. It forced me to get out of whatever old thought processes I had and change for the better. The pain taught me something that pride wouldn't let me learn.

For example, how many of us were told not to touch the stove because it and the fire were hot? After it was mentioned, all you could think of was touching the stove even after being told not to. Then you believed (with pride), the stove wasn't hot and didn't want you to have fun. So, when you did, you screamed in pain and ran to the person who told you not to touch it. This means you thought you knew better, and the pain from touching the stove humbled and hurt you, teaching you faster than the instruction given.

What God has and is continuing to do for me is grow, help, nurture, guide, and heal me. I saw God, and you can never unsee God once you see God. Part of my healing and healing my heart was discovering within myself areas that needed healing. I have learned about the eight dimensions of wellness from my spiritual father, Bishop A. Bernard Hector. Before then, I had never heard about the eight dimensions of wellness. We function daily through the eight dimensions of wellness: emotional/mental, physical, occupational, social, spiritual, intellectual, environmental, and financial *(Stoewen, 2017)*. How we function in these dimensions of wellness impacts our quality of life.

The three dimensions of wellness that most impacted my healing heart journey were mental/emotional, physical, and spiritual. I realized these areas needed the most healing attention to flow and fully experience the other areas of wellness as a perfect, whole, and complete person of God *(Philippians 4:7 KJV)*. To reach my full potential and the purpose that God has designed for my life, I need to understand how these three areas of wellness create my foundation for growth and well-being. I will define the three dimensions of wellness for the book's purpose.

Mental/Emotional is understanding and respecting your feelings, values, and attitudes and feeling positive and enthusiastic about your life *(Stoewen, 2017)*. Physical is recognizing the need for physical activity, diet, sleep, and nutrition *(Swarbrick, 2012)*. Spiritual is expanding our sense of purpose and meaning in life *(Swarbrick, 2012)*. In the coming chapters, I will delve deeper into these areas and what healing looked like for me. For now, let's speak to the realizations and processes I underwent.

I realized this foundational work required me to be brutally honest, owning every part I played in my life, and facing some of my harder truths. I had to accept that this included areas of my life that I thought I had conquered. I needed to revisit these core foundational moments of my life. The mental, physical, and spiritual side of myself, I believed, were intact until I was in situations that resembled past experiences. I could not see my behavior patterns. I began my journey towards healing my heart to be better for myself and my relationship with God so that I could love others in a healthy, healed way.

For example, I previously believed I truly misunderstood what it meant to love myself until I came across people with the old patterns of behavior that led me back into those same cycles of feeling unworthy, and unvalued. Those types of people were depressed, toxic, and demeaning to me. I believed once I stated my boundaries, people would hear me and wouldn't cross them. That was not the case, in turn, they tested my limits, and I didn't enforce my boundaries, leaving me feeling worthless and invalidated. Let's discuss and define the Healing Heart's journey and what a healed heart is. **Healing** is the process of making or becoming sound or being healthy again. **Heart** is the central or innermost part of a person that helps us connect with others. The characteristic of a healed heart is that a **Healed Heart** can live a holistic, healthy, perfect, whole, and complete life and genuinely connect with others *(Psalm 47:3)*. So, let's dig into the three areas mentioned.

> *"He heals the and binds up their wounds."*
>
> ~PSALM 147:3 (NKJV)

CHAPTER ONE

Mental/Emotional

> *"...for he is the kind of person who is always thinking about the cost. "Eat and drink," he says to you, but his heart is not with you."*
>
> ~PROVERBS 23:7 (NIV)

I am a person who is capable of owning what she sees and understands about herself. However, events from childhood to adulthood caused me to autocorrect, which skewed my view of seeing and participating in life's events. What I mean by this is that what happened only showed me the world's view of love, communication or lack thereof, relationships, and a host of other things that were not healthy. For example, I was exposed to emotionally dysregulated adults in childhood who could not regulate their emotions, and I thought it was normal. Emotional dysregulation is an emotional response inadequately controlled in an accepted range of emotional reactions (APA, 2022).

What a deregulated adult looked like to me was a person who could not control their mood; the communication was dysfunctional such as yelling, extreme temper outbursts, and tantrums including (verbal and nonverbal), and other over-the-top behaviors *(APA, 2022)*. A dysregulated person/adult is a person who may also exhibit chronic irritability and trouble dealing with internal stress and outside stressors. They may not have the ability to regulate their mood, anxiety, and emotions. This means they are not operating in a place of calmness, stability, thought processes, and emotional intelligence to convey messages and instruction. They appear to be all over the place and for a child (like me), I didn't know what to do with that and internalized their inability as being my fault.

Dysregulated people/adults can't operate from a place of regulation because they do not at the time have the capability and capacity to handle the current situation they may be facing. So, when someone talked to me while they were dysregulated, I would "speak on it", only to get shut down, believing it would be over soon. I would shut down because I did not know what to do, I did not (and still don't) like arguing. I wanted to talk about the issue(s) and for everything to be calm. I often felt like I was walking on eggshells. I did not want to do that, but as a result, I was.

In my mind, as a child, I believed that spending time with the person was more important than the disagreement. I didn't know this then, but I learned how to shut down when this happened to me. Maybe some of you have experienced this in your life where you wanted the connection with the person more than arguing over something you wouldn't even remember in 6 hours. If so, let me introduce myself. "Hi, I am Tam, and I am a card-carrying member, and it is nice to meet you." I will be taking you on a healing heart journey with me, and prayerfully, you will gain some tips to help you on your healing heart journey.

What happened to me flowed through most of my life, and it depended on the person when I would not shut down. I learned to stand up for myself, but no one taught me how to deal with people who have unregulated emotions. Basically, I did not have strong boundaries to protect myself. I always did my best to respect others, hoping for the same in return, as I never intended to mistreat anyone. I was trying to speak up, fight for myself, and be heard. What I now come to understand with God's help and therapy is that when those moments arose, and I shut down, the inner child in me needed protection. That shutdown was a defense mechanism against the trauma I experienced.

Now that you know a little more about me and some of the mental trauma I experienced from my past, we can transition into discussing trauma and what kind of effects it may have had on you into adulthood. I know we all like to say traumatic experiences did not change us, but they did! Little by little, the more you are traumatized from any of life's events and do not truly heal from it, the more you are allowing more pain to build on top of the original source of pain. So, the mind takes on the hurt and forces you to see things from that view until you do the work to change your perspective mentally.

The mind knows how to hold on to what it needs to survive. It is an example of muscle memory. However, if you learned bad habits and had to make decisions in survival mode, then the brain will pull on what it knows, even the bad/negative things you learned. Since those things helped you before, the mind, which controls the body, will use what it recalls surviving. It is imperative that we understand how we move in the world, and what we think drives how we do what we do. This is why healing your heart in the three areas previously mentioned is what I believe to be the core foundation for aligning oneself to living a perfect, whole, and complete life.

There are three areas in the mental aspect I discovered for myself that I needed to address: the mind, the heart, and the feelings. The mind is where we reference all our memories and experiences to help us make decisions. The heart is where we communicate our desires and passions about those decisions. The feelings are where we decide to or not to accept and agree with our heart and mind. This is why our mind, heart, and feelings dictate how we judge ourselves, our surroundings, and our emotions. These three areas will be broken down specifically for further clarity and insight.

Mind

In *Proverbs 23:7 KJV*, the word states "So a person thinketh, so are they," which means whatever you have allowed or accepted as a base thought or principle for yourself, you will believe until you change it. That means I had to find out why I was thinking the way I was about life, people, and the events that happened to or around me. In "The King's Domain Kingdomology 101", what we think of ourselves is how we behave or be. It is in the mind that we must accept and take accountability for our actions, behaviors, and responses (Hector & Pulley, 2021). This is a part of our way of thinking, speaking, being, and behaving mentally. Through this process, we can change how we think about ourselves, people, and events happening to us. When we operate with a dysfunctional way of thinking, we lose the opportunity to take accountability and ownership in what we do and how we move in life with ourselves, people, and events.

Accountability forces us to accept the truth about how we acted towards ourselves, behaved with people, and responded to life's events. Now the task becomes to change and challenge ourselves to think differently and better of ourselves, people, and the events that happen to us. We must recognize our pattern of behavior. I am certain that while reading the statement, we must acknowledge our pattern of behavior; some of you may have scoffed at the idea and believe that you do not have a pattern and that things are happening to you because everything and everyone else is wrong. I assure you that we all have ways our minds recall things that have worked for us before, and that is why we go back to them again for an expected outcome; hence, we have behavior patterns.

Another example of having a pattern is if you have ever asked yourself why things keep happening to you, and you do not understand why. Chances are you have been performing or doing something that keeps you in a perpetual cycle. We see the need for accountability and change in the ownership of our thought patterns. Taking responsibility for our behavior means accepting there are things you do not like about yourself. This is a prime indicator that the real heart works mentally and stems from the belief system that probably developed during childhood. Your belief system that was created from trauma and unhealed issues skewed how you see yourself, and people, and experience life events.

Those childhood events and traumas during our developmental phase skewed our thoughts and impacted our ability to trust and communicate with ourselves and others. It also affected how we interpreted our experiences. To be clear, there is a difference between people and experiences. For example, I believed people and experiences were grouped together, and because of that, I made my decisions about people and experiences the same.

How did I come to see that people and experiences were different? They are different because people are independent and are not always responsible for the experience because they are there. I had to realize that the people and the experience are different. People are not responsible for triggers that happened to me (you), and I (you) for reacting to past traumas. From a healed perspective, others may be experiencing a dysregulated version of you. Whenever you cannot recognize what you are dealing with and cannot isolate your pattern of behavior, you should sit down and begin to evaluate your thoughts and talk with God. Examples of talking with God can be journaling, prayer, and meditation. Ask God for discernment about your problems and get therapy to uncover what happened to you.

If you can do this and stay committed to God, the process, and a therapist, you will be able to find out where the issues and pattern (s) of behavior came from to get to the root of the problem. We use our discernment with God by meditating, journaling, and sitting in the stillness and silence long enough for the Spirit of God to reveal to us what to do. Then, get direction and pray for the perfect counselor to help you navigate this healing journey. Once you have the root of the issue, you will learn more about yourself and how to defeat those old ways of thinking and behavior patterns through supplication and prayer. It would be best to surround yourself with positivity and journal daily to get those negative thoughts out of your head. Start with dancing, singing, and crying, and all positive devices to help you think better and believe better about yourself, people, and life's events.

After I meditate, I write down what I feel and think, listen to music, and dance with my dog to relieve stress and negative thoughts. I use positive affirmations about myself and what God says about me in scripture. One scripture I use is Psalm 139. I also use Isaiah 43:1 "For I am his, and He is mine." I refute negative thoughts with scripture. I recount the many times God has shown me favor and love throughout my life. I remember who I am in Christ. Other than scripture, I also use this personal statement, "the truth needs no proof". You don't need to jump through hoops to prove yourself. Let the truth stand, and the rest fall. You can use anything that keeps you from meditating on depressive thoughts and behaviors.

Surround yourself with positive conversations while working on healing the inner child in you to help heal the adult. Celebrate yourself and every win, no matter how big or small. If you paid rent, bought yourself a shirt, took a much-needed break from work, or did not answer a phone call when you did not want to, tell yourself, "You did a good job."

Find out what your triggers are. Knowing your triggers enables you to heal better mentally by spotting them and learning how to adjust yourself. You begin to ask healthier questions for your mental state, such as, do I need to be here in this place, do I want to go, or even do I need to respond? Identifying the triggers also helps you avoid negative and intrusive thoughts for you to beat depressive symptoms and thoughts.

For me, I recognized that when I was going through the events of life, the intrusive and negative thoughts hit harder and came to my mind often. Whatever I thought about myself, I merely manifested it into my life by thinking about it incessantly. If I believed anything negative and accepted it as a fact, I believed it and moved accordingly. Negativity can spread faster than wildfire because you are experiencing hurt, guilt, and shame about what happened to you, especially if you don't understand why you are doing what you do. The intrusive/negative thoughts were intense and frequent as I tried to tell myself those thoughts were not true. None of it is true; it is ALL a mind game, and you are the one who decides how you play it.

Examples of intrusive/negative thoughts are when you tell yourself that no one wants to be your friend, and you never thought that before. Alternatively, if you call someone normally, it doesn't bother you if they don't answer, and they get back to you later. The mind in a hurt view will say 'See, they don't love you. If they did, they would have answered you." However, the truth is that other people have things going on, and the person always calls you back when they have time. This is the time you really pull on scripture, pray, journal, sit in silence, and ask God to reveal to you what is happening with you.

Here is a prime opportunity for you to have an experience with God. You are co-creating with God the purpose for your life, what God has for you, and the desires of your heart. One must understand that believing in your mind means accepting and agreeing to what you are thinking. This is the basis of how you will move on or towards an action.

What was true was God's unconditional love for me. God's thoughts of me are lovely, and I am made in God's likeness and image. These are some of the things I said to myself while on my mental healing journey. I also read the Bible even more, continued therapy, and made extra visits during the week when needed. I accepted what needed to be changed mentally, which led to my heart and what work needed to be done.

For example, when I attended therapy, I talked about what I discovered in meditation with God and addressed the issues I have with self-worth, self-esteem, parenting myself, and pouring love back into me that I was seeking from others. I found out as an adult the love I needed was always in me. God and my therapist helped me genuinely see me and accept the right, wrong, indifference, and everything about me.

Therapy helped me to see that I was exposed to dysregulated adults/people and toxic situations I should have never seen nor heard as a child. This is when I began to parent myself. Parenting myself looks like me sharing with myself everything I needed and wanted to hear when I was young. Basically, what would I have liked to have known or have been told as a child growing up? How would I comfort myself? Also, asking why or what is triggering me so I control my emotional state to speak clearly and express my needs.

Heart

The heart of the matter for me mentally is that I recognized that healing in this area affected my heart and how I saw myself, people, and life's events. The heart drives a person to do everything and brings with it all the passion needed to complete it. No one will ever do something wholeheartedly that they are not passionate about. Passion is the driving force in what we do because we believe it wholeheartedly. So, healing the heart is what we must do to align and change what we think. We do this by destressing and healing our hearts through forgiveness, meditating on God's word day and night, journaling (I can't stress that enough), and seeing our counselor regularly.

In this, I learned I am a giver; as a giver, my boundaries must be very strong in a world full of takers. When I say that I am a giver, that means I am a person who cares for others so much that I put the needs of others above my own. My giving came in the form of money, time, talent, and energy. For some, you may not be a giver, you may be a taker and takers are selfish in nature and only care about their needs and what benefits them. Takers will use the previously listed resources and more for their benefit to the disadvantage of a giver. As a taker, boundaries aren't your issue, empathy may be your issue. These are some examples of what you must realize about yourself when going through the healing heart's journey. This means during this introspective moment, I had to accept the hard truths about myself.

I had to learn how to understand my boundaries, and to apply them when I felt violated. What I needed to feel safe meant letting others know that I would not accept the behavior shown to me; and that I have a consequence for your violation up to and including my absence from your life to guarantee my safety and peace.

I had the opportunity to be a part of the Cup and Saucer Covenant with God. The cup and saucer covenant is a union between you and God, representing what is for you and others. The cup represents what God has blessed you with by the fruit of the spirit. These blessings are the fruits of the spirit: kindness, self-control, faithfulness, gentleness, joy, peace, love, patience, and many others *(Gal. 5:22-23)*. The saucer is what overflows from your cup that you can share and give to others, so you are not depleted. When you look at it, a cup is designed to hold specific items for the one using the cup. What falls out of the cup to the saucer can be given to others without taking away from what is in your cup. The cup has a boundary, and so does the saucer. I found it eye-opening during this healing process because God taught me about boundaries by applying this Cup and Saucer Covenant.

The Cup and Saucer Covenant taught me that I give only from my saucer, not my cup. I used to do that until I understood that I am a child of God and can still say, "No" and be holy. That doesn't mean I don't love you. It means protecting my heart and the things hidden in me until such a time calls my purpose forward. We all have boundaries and should stand firm on them, so we are not taken advantage of or left feeling empty emotionally, mentally, and/or spiritually. This means acknowledging and accepting what role you played in your life. I recognize the role I played in my life by allowing people to continue to run over my boundaries (childhood trauma), not knowing how to stop people who ran over my boundaries when they did, and forgiving myself when it happened. You are never to let anyone cross your boundaries. I was being nice and thinking that being quiet meant keeping the peace. Unfortunately, and gracefully, I learned that keeping the peace was detrimental to me until I realized whose peace I was holding, and it was not mine. I will never let anyone else's peace and joy come before mine ever again, and I will not let it happen again.

My Yays are my Yays, and my Nays are my Nays. We cannot give the benefit of the doubt to anyone, platonic or intimate, or otherwise, if they truly have not shown themselves honorable in their words and actions. If you haven't seen a true pattern of their actions matching what their words say, then the answer is No. So, despite what you think or may have seen in the movies, healing your heart for your mental well-being is not taking bubble baths (although nice occasionally), or drinking a glass of wine, and boom, your heart and mind are holistically together, and you can now conquer the world again.

Real heart healing, mentally, is not linear (no real healing is). It can be crying, yelling, cursing, praying, and asking yourself the tough questions. In that process, I also sought scripture to build up my heart's strength and spoke to myself about how God sees me in the image and likeness that I am. I continued to connect with positive energy and people with good conversations while removing myself from those who desire to reside in the "Oh woe is me" mindset.

It would be best to believe wholeheartedly in the mindset to change and start thinking good about yourself. That's what I did for myself to help propel myself further into God's loving arms and into Loving myself with impunity. I then truly understood what it meant to *speak those things that were not as though they were (Romans 4:17 KJV)*. I learned how to love myself by parenting myself from the past trauma that happened to me, with people, and life's events. The little girl (feminine energy) and little boy (masculine energy) in me needed me to be heard and validated; no one could do that for me, it was only God and myself. We all have both feminine and masculine energy, some present more feminine than others, and some present more masculine, regardless of self-identification. This makes us human, and we are all on God's spectrum. God is the author and finisher of our faith, so judgment of who we are resides with God. *(Hebrews 12:2 KJV)*.

I had to speak life into myself, and I know that can be a battle sometimes because it is literally you versus you in this moment. You have to conquer yourself. I discovered that part of my healing involves overcoming my mind's disruptive thoughts and nurturing myself so deeply that it will align with my soul to feed my spirit. This comes from the heart. Once you understand the battle from within is you vs. you then you must battle yourself and God.

Battling God means you understand that He is in control of your life. While He cannot force you to relinquish control, it requires your mutual consent to entrust your life to Him for guidance and protection. He is the author and finisher of your faith, and all good and perfect things come from Him *(Heb 12:2)*. Meaning to surrender everything you thought you expected of your life concerning you and your outcome to God. An example of this would be allowing God to present to you the desires He has for you, and not how you think your life should be.

When you accept God's being in control and follow God's divine direction for your life, all the things you have desired will follow. Matthew 6:33 indicates that seeking the Kingdom of God and His righteousness first, that all of the things you desire shall be added unto you. After you are fully aligned with God, you can battle with everyone else. Battling with everyone else means you are able to place issues in their proper place and not take them personally. Everything begins to make sense when you realize whatever was going on with that person is about them and not you. You can receive information from them differently and see what it is they want from you if you can assist them.

It is now the moment when the Supernatural Spirit of God can give you the true peace that surpasses all understanding. God's peace and understanding are the Fruits of the Spirit. This is what the Glory of God can do for you once you truly give in and let God be God over your life. I should know because God has and is still doing it for me. Others may see you as heartless, braggadocious, cocky, or whatever they have in mind. However, that doesn't matter now because it is what God said and has fortified with you in scripture and the Divine Protection that is over your life. What anyone else says doesn't matter *(Philippians 4:7 KJV)*.

Do you believe the self-acceptance and acknowledgment process will happen for you? That is a tough question to ask yourself. If you have difficulty facing this question, the deeper dive into the heart will become rougher as you seek the healing you so deserve. Let me ask you: Do you believe and pray that everyone else receives their healing before you? That seems easier to do as you believe wholeheartedly for someone else but not for yourself. As the young people say, the math aint mathing. The truth is you can't believe it for anyone else if you don't believe it for yourself. You are deserving of healing, peace, and all the Joy of the Lord. Believe!

Again, whatever you think and believe is driven by your heart, bringing your feelings/emotions to the table. I wear my feelings on my sleeves, and I know that is true because I spend a lot of time with myself. I have always been this way, and I tried to deny myself that level of vulnerability because so much trauma happened over the course of my life. I thought I had to be in protection mode instead of trusting God and the discernment inside me to allow God's Divine Protection and timing to gauge others' intentions toward me.

Feelings/Emotions

When it comes to your feelings/emotions relating to the mental, the heart, and healing, the alignment within yourself has to be as tight as the skin attached to your body. What I mean by that is when you think it, you start to believe it, and when you believe it, you again put your heart into it, and your feelings and emotions tag along, also. Then, we have what I call, how we show up in the world. For that reason, our feelings and emotions are what others experience when they encounter us. If we are unbalanced in our feelings/emotions, we tell those around us what we think, believe, and where we are at that moment. We lose an opportunity to build friendships and relationships because we aren't aligned with God and ourselves.

When we lose control of feelings/emotions or ourselves, even for a split second, it appears that there's no room for apologies when you have never done a thing to anyone other than receive them for who they are. When you have no ill intent towards anyone and you finally have an explosive moment emotionally, you get judged by the very same people you have supported and cared for. You may be expecting them to do the same for you. If that's not you, that's okay because that's what I thought in a very childlike way. My thoughts were, if I could take you as you are, you would do the same for me. I fell in love with a quote from Ralph Waldo Emerson,"*Who we are speaks so loudly I cannot hear what you say.*" This means that what we do action-wise speaks louder than any words we tell someone.

So, you must be a person of integrity in your feelings/emotions. Now, that is not to say that you are not human and cannot express yourself with passion when issues that are not right arise.

By all means, speak your mind; however, it is how we communicate our minds with our hearts. Our feelings/emotions are how we will be received, heard, and understood. As mentioned previously, some are committed to misunderstanding you. If this is the case, this example is separate from them. Individuals who are committed to misunderstanding means no matter what you say or try to explain, they will never hear, validate, or confirm what you know to be true. They will most likely gaslight and manipulate what you say to avoid accountability. You have to know when not to speak and when to speak. That comes from life experiences and exposure to different types of personalities. That was a "Tam's Tidbit" for you right there.

As it relates to the alignment of your mind and your heart, your feelings/emotions as healing oneself, we must understand that they all flow together as a complete package delivered to the world. With that said, ask yourself, do you like how you are showing up in the world? There were times I could say I didn't like how I showed up in the world. I was actually sick of myself, holding myself back, stunting who I was for others to shine, holding back my intelligence level, and looking for validation in people and things that could never satisfy me. When I spent more time with God and my therapist, I recognized my past traumatic childhood.

What that looked like was me being sick of allowing people to use me. Why was the same cycle of events happening to me? I was left to start over from the bottom again in friendships, relationships, and any other "ships" I ventured into. I found myself often wondering why God. I had more questions than answers. It was not until this healing journey, that God stepped in and answered me. It was when I was alone and still.

God delivered me from the foolishness I was doing regarding my value, letting me know that I am enough and that I AM perfect, whole, and complete as His child. God revealed to me my heavenly name and showed me who I am in Him. God confirmed that I was born with the authority given to me to be the head and not the tail. That means I walk in everything the Lord has for my life. I desire to live this life and live it more abundantly. It is our birthright as children of the Most High.

The goal here is to show you how detailed we were created in God's image and how the connections from one area of our life lead to another. The Father skillfully crafted us; each and every one of us is a unique divine expression of the Most High. I desire to show how interconnected we all are to God, ourselves, and other people to show up in the world. This comes in the form of being mentally intact and functioning on all levels, holistically and authentically in the world.

If you don't accept that you need healing, but everyone can have it, you have denied the process of healing for you. The goals of the Kingdom are to Love God, Love Yourself, and then Love Everybody Else *(Pulley, 2019)*. You deserve healing and a prosperous life; you belong to God, and casting your cares on Him means you realize that you too can receive healing because you know that God cares for you fully. Believing it for yourself is the first step to valuing yourself. You must engage God every day and in every situation. When we have encounters, we can see the hand/manifestation of God in our lives and trust in the source (God) to show us the way. That now leads us to the Physical area of healing our hearts.

CHAPTER TWO

Physical

"Do you not know that your bodies are temples of the Holy Spirit, who is in you, whom you have received from God? You are not your own; you were bought at a price. Therefore honor God with your bodies."

~1 CORINTHIANS 6:19-20 (NIV)

The physical portion of heart healing involves the body's activity and functionality. We see this in scripture as the Kingdom of God is inside of us, as referenced in (Luke 17:20-21). In the book The King's Domain: Kingdomology 101, Bishop A. Bernard Hector describes four major definitions of Kingdom. Each definition covers God's unique governance over certain domains. For this book, I will use the third definition as it relates to the physical functionality of the body. God's Kingdom system is a system or form of government, meaning a way of being, seeing, thinking, speaking, and behaving (Hector & Pulley, 2021).

The body houses our soul and spirit, which helps present our way of being, seeing, speaking, moving, and behaving. Examples are seeing yourself as whole, well, healed, joyful, and peaceful and believing you can have it in your physical form. Do you see yourself as whole, well, healed, joyful, and peaceful? Let us dive into the body's physical healing and the areas to cover.

In this healing area, we will cover three issues: the eyes, body image, and overall physical health. Working on the physical aspect of healing may bring up different triggers or concerns for most. I know it did for me. When I experienced a great extreme amount of stress, my body held onto that experience and pain. My body wasn't relaxed enough to get rid of the tension, stressful, toxic, and painful energy it needed to release to heal. My body stored up that negative energy that happened to it and I needed it gone. My body needed to be healthy, so I could run my race, and live out my God-given purpose for my life *(1 Corinthians 9:24-27 KJV)*.

The best I can describe a stressed-out physical form is stiffness, pain, tight and sore muscles, and unexplained sickness. The body remembers the emotional pain. The body is designed to free what does not serve it by releasing waste. This means the body is never to hold anything that works against itself. As it relates to the eyes, body image, and health of the body, I will lay out how each of these areas manifested to me and how it aligns with your heart being healed. The eyes are the windows to the soul; therefore, we see what can alter who we are if we look at the world through hurt lenses *(Matthew 6:22-23 KJV)*.

What we see affects our thought process, leading to our heart, feelings/ and emotions. If we see the world through negativity, we will only see negativity. However, we will see positivity if we choose to heal ourselves and see the world through positivity. We must decide how we want to show up and see the world through our eyes, present ourselves physically, and through optimal health.

Eyes

While on my healing journey, I experienced an eye issue where I was isolated and home worshipping. God isolated me because I didn't see things correctly. I was looking at the world through hurt lenses. God decided that was the time for us to have a supernatural encounter and an encounter like no other. God spent time with me through prayer, journaling, silence, and stillness of what was happening to me. God didn't want me to go out and compromise myself and my life's purpose because my heart was broken, and I didn't know how to fix it. It was good that I was afflicted because my heavenly father revealed himself and protected me from me *(Psalms 119:71 KJV)*.

I will never forget what I experienced; it changed my life forever. During this intimate exchange, I could hear with my heart what God was truly trying to show me about myself. God showed me what needed attention so I would not repeat any old patterns in my life that no longer worked. I had a faulty vision concerning those childhood problems. Those problems were the original root of my defective eyesight (physically and spiritually). I took that information from God to my therapist and targeted the problem areas to resolve: unhealed places, scars, and trauma. It was the best thing God did because real healing took place in my life for the first time.

I had been in therapy for years and healed from other issues, yet I found myself not fully recovered from specific issues from childhood and did not know how to get to the root of it. God, being my creator, showed me my pattern of behavior that kept me repeating previous cycles that did not serve me. That doesn't mean those issues won't come back; it just means I know how to identify them. Once I can identify that it's toxic for me, I need to practice what I learned spiritually and in therapy to put those things in their proper place so I can continue my healing heart journey.

This is how I found out what my triggers were and what I needed to do to parent myself. I could truly see because God sat me down spiritually with the issues concerning my eyes. My mother used to tell me that maybe it had to hurt you for you to see. As painful as that was, I was able to see. Isn't it funny how pain will teach you something that pride won't let us learn another "Tam's Tidbit" for you?

Now, with the healing of my eyes both spiritually

and physically, I am back aligned to how I should see the world because I am better now with enhanced vision. My vision has been enhanced mentally, physically, and spiritually. Targeting the body image issues and what you may want to look like in your head is another factor in this process.

Body Image

Body image issues are something that most of us can relate to. We may want our thighs to be smaller, our hips to be larger, a different skin tone, our muscles to be larger, or even a different eye color. We could point out so many things being wrong with us. Why do we not focus on what is right with us? What the world deemed beautiful has placed us all in self-degradation. We began to hate what we saw in the mirror. We started tearing down the wonderful creation we are in God.

Body image issues stem most times from low self-esteem and a lack of value in oneself. The inner work begins with loving everything you see about yourself and everything you do not. The lack of validation and value may have originated from childhood or maybe as you age.

Low self-esteem places you in a place of vulnerability for negative thoughts and others' perspectives of you to come in and change the beautiful creation you are.

You begin to devalue yourself and lower the boundaries you may have set for yourself about what you will not accept from anyone for the sake of having someone or being accepted by others. Some may have undergone body modification procedures to change their appearance to what we think is beautiful. The value comes from God, and then you value yourself. Valuing yourself is the assurance that you are setting strong boundaries and not appearing needy. It stops you from hearing someone else's voice to be louder than God's voice in your head. God and your voice should be the loudest voices regarding you.

Listening to anyone else's voice opens space for you to be disconnected from God. That disconnection or separation between you and God hurts you and Him as it affects your self-image. What happened in the disconnection causes issues because you believed someone else and not God. God is the one who created you in likeness and image. This means that if we take what anyone else says about us and begin to hate our image, we are slapping

God in the face.

We just told God that what He created is not good enough. However, we should have realized we were perfect and complete the entire time. We did not need to change our looks. We needed to change our hearts towards ourselves and our creator. God chose our parents and the family we would be in. There was something specific from your father and your mother that created you; You needed that combination so you could be the unique individual expression in the earth *(Genesis 1:26 KJV)*.

What happened is that we bought into the world's system or version of what beauty should be and removed God from the equation. God is the one who created us in his likeness and image, and yet we are seeking the world's opinion of us. It is what we think of ourselves; no one else's opinion matters concerning your looks and presentation. The validation needed now would be daily affirmations in the mirror and repeating that God sees me, loves me, created me, and calls my name daily. God told me to use those phrases and words when we communed.

Speaking well of yourself is a form of self-care. Self-care is taking care of you in all aspects of your life, especially your body and physical performance. How we see ourselves manifests in how we visually see and love our bodies. The other way the body or physical form matters is how we treat our bodies. Taking care of ourselves means going to the doctor, taking meds (if needed), getting physical exams, and exercising.

Healthy Body

The body we have is a holy temple created by God to help us fulfill our purpose on earth. The ability to love yourself physically through exercise and doctor visits means you value yourself. You value the quality of life you have. You desire to be here and present on the earth. What these practices do is help release the stress that the body holds. Physical activity helps decrease anxiety and depression as it helps the body release the natural endorphins that increase happiness and joy. You feel better and have more energy, which calms your mind.

Physical issues we experience through life's events get trapped in the muscle tissue, and again, you begin feeling the stiffness, tiredness, soreness, and other painful problems the body is holding onto. Physical activity can help reduce those issues and release negative energy in the body. Working out also allows time to be quiet and commune with God. It allows time for thoughts to be processed successfully and not in an emotional state.

The physical body endures a lot, and we must be mindful to take care of it so that we may live long and be prosperous in the life God has given us. On the physical healing journey, I learned that all of the factors in this section were crucial in my healing. I was able to lose weight and foster a closer relationship with my creator and body to stay in alignment for optimal health. I see that my body is a holy temple and that God does desire the relationship and closeness through working out, that I tried to find in people, places, and other things *(1 Corinthians 6:19-20 KJV)*. The full alignment of the Mental and Physical ties into the Spiritual.

The Spiritual connection brings all the factors and points on the healing journey into a relationship with God. The spiritual aspect reveals if you are having encounters or experiences with God. Trust me, there is a difference between an encounter with the Father and having experiences with Him. Let us look deeper into the spiritual component of the continuous healing heart journey. The spiritual chapter will cover three specific focus areas for the healing journey.

The areas of the spiritual component regarding healing will be the spirit, soul, and supernatural experiences versus supernatural encounters with God. God is spirit, and we must worship God in spirit and in truth, for the father seeketh such for those who worship God *(John 4:23-24 KJV)*. I desire to convey what God has shown me on my healing journey and share what I learned with you.

Now, you get to decide to commune with God; one has to agree to walk with God and follow the example set by Jesus, our Wayshower *(Pulley, 2019)*. Jesus, our Wayshower, showed us how to live a fully human and divine life *(Pulley, 2019)*. Jesus perfectly balances humanity and divinity *(Pulley, 2019)*. As we are on the healing journey, this means that we are to be holistically healthy and balanced to have a life more abundantly *(John:10-10 KJV)*. In order to help you achieve the maximum healing of your heart, it will allow you full access to receive all the goodness of God because how can two walk together unless they agree *(Amos 3:3 KJV)*. If a person chooses not to agree to walk with God, in this healing heart journey, one can expect not to have supernatural experiences and encounters with God due to a lack of understanding.

CHAPTER THREE

Spiritual

"I and the Father are one."

JOHN 10:30 (NIV)

God desires a relationship with you. It is a mutual exchange of love, peace, joy, longsuffering, and other wonderful benefits of being in relation with God (Galatians 5:22-23 KJV). It is believing what you experience with God; God will be revealed to you in those supernatural encounters and collective experiences. In addition, it is in those supernatural experiences and encounters that you see yourself in God. Now, the question is, do you desire supernatural experiences or encounters with God? We will explore the spirit, soul, and supernatural experience versus supernatural encounters with God.

On my healing journey, I had the opportunity to invite God into every situation I faced. Did I do it all of the time? No. The reason is that sometimes I get so caught up in my head and the pain of what I am going through that I do not remember to call on God. When I did catch my breath and slowed my breathing down, I called on God and began to pray for help. I am very curious, so I ask many questions, and every time I ask God a question, I receive the answer in the form of a life event and experience that grew me, or I read it in scripture. I learned that not only does God answer, but God is waiting for me to commune with Him in spirit regularly. Sometimes, I did not include God, I made a decision, and I did not pray and ask God if this was what I was supposed to be doing. I found myself in some sticky situations that hurt me, and even through that, God still helped me because I asked when things got rough.

Had I asked initially instead of in the middle of the problem, I would have been spared the grief. This is something I learned on my healing journey with God.

It is God's desire that I engage in conversation in every situation, decision, and problem to help decrease the amount of hurt you will experience. That does not mean that some things will not happen to you because we need certain things to happen for our souls to grow in spirit and with God.

Spirit

On my journey in life, I have experienced public humiliation by others. An example of what that looked like for me was being cursed out in front of others and not reacting and having my name drug through the mud by those who wish to smear my name with untruths. For others, you may have experienced other forms of public shaming. There were those who, for whatever reason, saw me as a threat to them and their way of life. I know that I am a genuine person. I was once told that I hold a mirror up to people that forces them to see themselves. Those people did not like themselves and tried to tear me down.

For me, being publicly humiliated led to an embarrassing public crucifixion; I suffered like Jesus in a sense because I felt the weight and judgment of those whom I loved and left feeling the loss. I was devastated and continued my path with Jesus. Therefore, I picked up my cross with vigor and continued following Jesus, my Wayshower. Whenever you decide to pick up your cross and follow Jesus to some degree, you should expect some form of public humiliation, and you should also expect God to show up and help heal and resurrect you as you continue to complete your life's journey *(Tam's Tidbit)*.

Resurrection is restoration; examples include journaling, praying, sitting in silence, and awaiting a response from God. Other examples of resurrection are deciding not to give up and continue living because you are assured that greater days are ahead *(Haggai 2:9, Romans 8:18)*. God will always restore your broken heart so that you can genuinely heal. Restoration is not sadness, depression, anxiety, low self-esteem, or the like. It is joy and peace and walking with your head held high. For I know that whatever Jesus did, I can do, and can go through *(Pulley, 2019)*. This means the resurrection from whatever tried to hurt or destroy you propelled you into a rebirth. After each situation, I fell, and scripture tells us a just person falls seven times, and God receives the glory

(Proverbs 24:16 KJV).

So, what is a spiritual connection with God? It is the ability to co-create the life you deserve and desire with God *(Pulley, 2022)*. It is the ability to talk with God about everything you do. The closest example I can think of is talking to God like you're talking to someone in your face. we do not have to wait to talk to God. We can speak to God anywhere; we don't have to wait until we are completely alone to talk to Him. Instead, try talking with God in your room, car, on the job, in the park, or wherever you can release any negative thoughts to receive the goodness of God. God is omnipresent (is everywhere), omnipotent (has all power), and omniscient (knows all things), meaning God is wherever you are when you are and knows what is in your spirit, and that you need to release it.

Everything we do with conviction is derived from the spirit *(John 16: 7-11 NIV)*. The spirit leads to a higher level of consciousness where we believe greater about ourselves, think better of ourselves, and move better regarding ourselves. We must choose each day whether to be negative or positive *(Joshua 24:15 NIV)*. I always believed that whatever you think about yourself is what it is; if you think you will fail, then you will, but if you believe you are winning, then you are. We must remember that we actively participate in our self-development and growth. We do not have to sit down and take it. We must rise to the occasion and heal ourselves *(Luke 4:23 NIV)*. We speak life to ourselves. We tell ourselves that we can make it, that we are God's namesake, and as such, we are entitled to everything that God has for us *(Psalm 23:3 KJV)*.

We must worship God in spirit and in truth; this is the essence of who we are before God. This means telling God the truth about yourself and everything that happened in your life *(John 4:24 KJV)*. Although God is the author and finisher of our faith, it is in the trust of communication we invite God into our lives more intimately. God does desire a relationship with you, people who truly know us may already know that something has happened to us, yet, they still want to hear it from you. That is how God is about you, it is the acknowledgment that He is concerned about you. Including God in your spiritual process means you acknowledge His presence in your life. Spiritually, we are bound to someone and something, and that someone and something is God. Go boldly before the throne and cast your cares on God. Doing this takes the anxiety, depression, and low self-esteem off you and places it back where it belongs. It belongs with God the creator, not on us; God's yoke is light. That is why we cast all of our cares on him. God replaces it and restores you with joy, peace, love, kindness, grace, and mercy all fruits of the Spirit.

Soul

The soul is our consciousness, where we house our needs and emotions. As you see with the soul, the emotions from the mental aspect discussed beforehand may be coming together a little clearer now. Along this healing heart journey, all of us must admit that we have a soul, and to become who God purposed us to be and what we desire to become has to advance. It is in the awareness of our character that we open ourselves up to be taught. Where we put our faith and trust in God to help develop us. On the healing journey, it does not always work out that way. We have events in life that shift how we think.

Unfortunately, we learn to block ourselves off, stop trusting people, and block God out. We do not open up through life's events due to a lack of trust, and our soul gets stuck in what happened to us. This brings up previous muscle memory and those experiences. What that looked like for me was going into my head, not knowing if someone would be there for me. I did not call on God until things got so bad, because I thought I could do it on my strength. However, when I am weak, God is strong, and I am made whole *(2 Corinthians 12:9-11 NIV)*. Meaning that it is in my openness and vulnerability and what looks like weakness to others that God's grace is sufficient. God supplies all of my needs because I got out of my own way. I gave it all over to God. I had no more plans I could try or people to call, and God revealed that He is my source and always has and will be.

How can the soul prosper if we do not let God in to teach us? The short answer to this question is that we cannot. The original plan for our soul's unfolding and progress is to go to God first. Allowing God his rightful place as head of our lives lets His will be known unto you. The source from whom all blessings flow provides resources in the form of people to help you on your journey. These people will be fruitful in spirit and truthful in all actions concerning you. Those individuals came to solidify what God's plans are for you and what you have desired for yourself, without a fight or stress. That process will be easy and flow as easily as possible because anything with God is not a struggle or fight.

Supernatural Experience vs. Supernatural Encounter

The gifting and purpose in this life are greater than those who seek to destroy you. Although scripture tells us that a just person falls seven times, it never mentions what those falls would look like. The example of a just person is one who displays all of the fruits of the Spirit and is a good person. A just person contributes to society and is morally upright or good. Because of this, we must look at all of it as an orchestrated move of God. You rose again after the incident, and God received the glory because the lesson and blessing from the fall propelled you further into your relationship with God. After all, you prayed and sought God for help.

These are growing pains; we have all heard that phrase before; however, did you understand what that means or looks like? Growing *(adj.)* means becoming greater over a period of time; increasing. Pain *(noun)* means careful effort, great care, or trouble. Together, I came up with this definition of growing pains, which means the act of becoming greater over a period of time with careful and great care regarding the troubles in life. The definition fits because we are walking with God, and the race is not given to the swift *(Ecclesiastes 9:11 KJV)*.

This means with prayer and praying without ceasing, you will gain true wisdom and knowledge of God through your experiences and encounters with God over time. Supernatural experiences and supernatural encounters help develop the very nature and character of who you are to be. Asking God for knowledge, wisdom, and instruction is not a weakness *(John 14:27 KJV)*.

What do experiences and encounters mean on the healing journey? How do they relate to you and God? I seek to answer those questions because I wanted to understand the difference. An experience *(verb)* is defined as having experience of undergoing. Furthermore, undergoing means a transformation. Encounter means *(verb)* to come upon or experience, especially unexpectedly. To explain the difference between my supernatural experiences with God and me meant that I went through a transformation process every time we spent together through the growing pains.

My supernatural experiences with God were completely different from the supernatural encounters. My supernatural experiences with God all come from me setting aside dedicated time to meditate, journal, sing, dance, worship with, and praise God. These were times that I ensured I spent with God before life intervened. When life's events hit you, sometimes it comes in waves, and you become distracted from spending time with God and centering yourself. When we are in a calmer state of consciousness, we move differently. Our days are truly better. The supernatural experience is daily and all the time, not sporadic in nature. There is constant communication between the creator and you.

This is the very space that God loves to be in with you because you are focused on your relationship with yourself and God. You align yourself with truth and purpose and create healthy, holistic, well-rounded relationships. So, the supernatural experiences are constantly engaging with God regularly. No one's opinions of you will matter, and therefore, nothing will be able to move you off your solid foundation with God. Meaning the supernatural experiences resonate on a far greater scale than my supernatural encounters with God.

My supernatural encounters with God over my life were so unexpected, and they came upon me quickly. For example, I was diagnosed with breast cancer in 2012 on my birthday (ironically), and I was driving from Annapolis to Glen Burnie, Maryland. That was about a 20 to 25-mile ride. I was headed to my doctor's appointment and running late. I was driving at least 65 to 70 mph. When I pulled over in the parking lot, my front right axle broke on my car, and it collapsed there. That was an example of God's Divine Protection over my life and one amazing supernatural encounter.

For me, supernatural encounters with God come upon you quickly through prayer or circumstances that require an immediate response. You may need assistance right away and prayer directly represents God's power. For a person building trust in God as a newcomer to faith and kingdom; I believe this is God's initial way of letting you know He is there and has always been, just on a much smaller scale. God being there on a much smaller scale does not equate to the awesome power He has. It is a reflection of someone who is not fully aware of God's presence. This is an introduction to your faith and God's presence. I used the newcomer of faith as an example because they are learning how to trust God, build up their prayer life, and learn not to be so easily distracted by the events of life. I present this as a way of explaining why they may feel as though they are having supernatural encounters with God and not the full supernatural experiences in the knowledge of God. We tend to operate in the light in which we know. When we see more, we can do more.

A newcomer is a person/individual being introduced to God through Jesus Christ. A newcomer is a person who knows little to no information about God and the knowledge of God's presence. I am not a newcomer as I have been with God and Jesus for over 20 years. If you are not affiliated with a church body you are not discounted from the healing hearts journey, because God rains on the just as well as the unjust and your healing is still a part of your inheritance with God *(Matt. 5:45 NLV)*. Everyone has challenges and therefore still needs answers to life and life events.

    I specifically chose the verb definitions of each word because there is action taking place, and the action is between you and God. This exchange of spiritual connection changed my entire perspective on how God operates as a spiritual father. Through the supernatural experience of God, I am relegated to His will and not trying to control the outcome anymore. I fully accept and surrender to God's will and purpose for my life, and I can continue to receive the healing I need constantly. When I have encounters, I stop spending time with God and relying on my own intellect, allowing life and other people, places, and things to distract me from my healing. For me, the encounters take longer to bounce back from due to me relying on myself and not co-creating with God. However, it can be done: do not give up on God, and do not give up on yourself.

The supernatural experience versus the supernatural encounter related to God are the levels of trust you have with the creator. What I mean by that is this: we trust people daily to fix our food, take care of our families, and do a multitude of other things. Why can't we trust God for more than an encounter? I strive daily to seek God's face; we must try every day. We have a hard time trusting God to move on our behalf. Yet, we trust strangers to do things for us. We do that because those persons are readily identifiable when we want to put the blame on others. Since God is Spirit, people have a hard time fighting with a Spirit they can't see or touch. That is why we move by faith and not by sight when we are trusting God. Trust is the ultimate level of devotion, along with your faith. There is freedom in trusting God because you have time to think about other things that you are seeking to do. God knows the plans he has to prosper you.

Healing spiritually means not using band-aids to cover up superficial scratches, scars, and scrapes. Band-aids are temporary fixes to what may be deeper issues within yourself. Meaning for the healing heart journey band-aids cannot cover what is left of the heart. What healing looks like versus using a band-aid to cover up the scratches, scars, and scrapes uncovers the issues of the heart or the residue/residual pain and reminders of what allowed you to become stuck in a place of not healing and fully releasing. Again, spiritual healing is a full submission to the spirit of God. Full submission to God expands your humility and compassion for others as you understand and heal yourself.

Every Human created by God is Healthy, Mentally (Whole), Physically (Complete), and Spiritually (Perfect); as Jesus, our way shower has revealed how we ought to love. Our way-shower explains how we should treat one another and ourselves. We must first Love God (Matthew 22:37), Love ourselves (Psalm 139:14, Ephesians 5:29, Proverbs 19:8, Mark 12:31), and Love everyone else (Leviticus 19:34, James 2:8) *(Pulley,2019)*. Who and what we will be in this life starts with acknowledging God's awesome and mighty power. Then, we continue through the examples set by Jesus, our Wayshower, to love everyone else. There is no greater representation of Love than for us first to Love God, ourselves, and everybody else.

CONCLUSION

Through the healing heart's journey process, know and understand that God will place you in isolation, placing a Divine hedge of protection around you to help you begin the healing process. Isolation from God is His way of giving you a pause button on life and a chance to reset. Isolation is not God's punishment. Although you may think it is, it is not. God revealed that to me through this journey. God's isolation is his Divine Protection so others do not have the opportunity to hurt you more than what has already happened. Isolation may feel lonely and painful, and it is intended to be so that you face yourself and the creator God. No one in this world is immune from life's events; therefore, we all have some healing to do in our hearts, another "Tam's Tidbit" I learned on this journey.

Through this process, God's Divine timing allows us to regroup and thoroughly examine ourselves to ask Him all of the questions we have in our heart and mind to reveal what patterns we have that kept us from healing those painful cycles we were in. those painful cycles that hurt us are what hold us back from God and his fullness. This means your becoming perfect, whole, and complete is delayed, and the vision you have for yourself will become frustrating. So, allow this time that God has set aside for you to reflect and truly begin healing your heart.

The healing heart's journey is continuous because as we live this life, there will be painful events that will teach us how to connect more with God, ourselves, and everyone else. This process aligns with God's perfect, whole, and complete image we were created in. God patiently awaits you to answer the call and sit on his heavenly couch for a spiritual therapeutic awakening with Him. God is waiting to connect or reconnect in a relationship so that you can be what he has designed and what you desire to be. All this heart work will open up God's promises (made to you) of Divine Provision, having everything supplied to you naturally and spiritually.

On this healing heart journey, I discovered through the mental, physical, and spiritual aspects that I was and can truly heal my relationship with myself and God. Anything that stops you from reaching and feeling joy, happiness, and God's righteousness needs to be checked. I encourage and empower you to go down that rabbit hole, accept God's invitation, and heal your heart. This journey is personal and very necessary so that you show up in the world you have always desired. Prayerfully and hopefully, after reading the Healing Hearts journey, you are inspired to work on yourself, heal your heart, and remove anything that stops you from being your best self.

In writing The Healing Hearts: A Continuous Journey book, I realized three things about myself that coexist and can coexist: I am happy, hurting, and healing all at the same time. The process for you may be different. However, many things can coexist as you heal. And in that understanding, I am assured that with your relationship with God, yourself, and self-preservation, you will be able to truly love others, knowing in the end that Love always wins!

AUTHORS BIO

Hi, my name is Tamara "Tam" Jackson. I am sharing with you all my healing journey, praying and hoping that it inspires you on a self-healing journey. If the lessons I have learned through my life encourage you, then I have done what I set out to do. That is to help others see that they too can be free and live a perfect, whole, and complete life filled with joy, peace, and love.

REFERENCES

American Psychiatric Association. (2022). Diagnostic and statistical manual of mental disorders (5th ed., text rev.). https://doi.org/10.1176/appi.books.9780890425787

Hector, A.B., Dr. Pulley, D. (2021). Kingdomology: The Kings Domain Kingdomology 101 Second Edition July 8, 2021

Dr. Pulley, D.R. (2010). Getting Rid of the Junk: In Preparation for The Keys

Dr. Pulley, D.R. (2021). Jesus The Heart of The Matter: The Master's Manifesto on What Matters Most Publisher: The C.O.T.E.K. Press (February 5, 2021)

Dr. Pulley, D.R. (2022). The Keys to The Kingdom: A Devotional Guide to Living A Holistically Healthy, Balanced And Well-Rounded Life

Dr. Pulley, D.R. (2022). *Kingdom Vernacular: Why We Say What We Say, Publisher*: The C.O.T.E.K. Press (February 17, 2023)

Dr. Pulley, D.R. (2019). Wayshower: A New View of Jesus Publisher: Divine House Books (February 5, 2019), ISBN-10: 179230160X ISBN-13: 978-1792301605

The Holy Bible (n.d) https://www.biblegateway.com/passage/?search=Psalm%20119&version=KJV

Merriam Webster's Dictionary (2023). https://www.merriam-webster.com/dictionary/experience#:~:text=%3A%20the%20fact%20or%20state

%20of,b

The National Institute of Mental Health. Last Reviewed: January 2023 Disruptive mood dysregulation disorder: The basics

Oxford Dictionary (2023). Copyright © 2023 Oxford University Press https://www.oed.com/

Ralph Waldo Emerson Quotes. (n.d.). BrainyQuote.com. Retrieved December 16, 2023, from BrainyQuote.com Web site: https://www.brainyquote.com/quotes/ralph_waldo_emerson_103408

Stoewen, D. L. (2017). Dimensions of wellness: Change your habits, change your life. *The Canadian Veterinary Journal*, *58*(8), 861-862. https://www.ncbi.nlm.nih.gov/pmc/articles/PMC5508938/

Swarbrick, M. (2012). A Wellness Approach to Mental Health Recovery. In Recovery of People with Mental Illness: Philosophical and Related Perspectives. Abraham Rudnick, (ed). Oxford Press. https://alcoholstudies.rutgers.edu/mapping-mental-health-dr-swarbrick-the-eight-wellness-dimensions/#:~:text=Swarbrick's%20'8%20Dimensions'%20model%20has,%2C%20Occupational%2C%20Environmental%2C%20Financial.

www.ingramcontent.com/pod-product-compliance
Lightning Source LLC
Chambersburg PA
CBHW070849160426
43192CB00012B/2372